MW00964604

EQUATIONS = equals

Joe Ross

GREEN INTEGER
KØBENHAVN & LOS ANGELES
2004

GREEN INTEGER BOOKS
Edited by Per Bregne
København / Los Angeles

Distributed in the United States by Consortium Book
Sales and Distribution, 1045 Westgate Drive, Suite 90
Saint Paul, Minnesota 55114-1065.
Distributed in England and throughout Europe by
Turnaround Publisher Services
Unit 3, Olmypia Trading Estate
Coburg Road, Wood Green, London N22 6TZ
44 (0)20 88293009

(323) 857-1115 / http://www.greeninteger.com

First Green Integer Edition 2004
Some of the poems in this volume were previously published in
*Green Zero, The Impercipient, lower limit speech, Membrane, Object Permanence,
O.blek, Texture,* and the *WWPH Anthology.* The author wishes to thank the
editors of these publications.

Design: Per Bregne
Typography: Kim Silva
Photograph of Joe Ross by Douglas Messerli
Copyright ©2004 by Douglas Messerli

LIBRARY OF CONGRESS CATALOGING IN PUBLICATION DATA
Joe Ross [1960]
EQUATIONS = equals
ISBN: 1-931243-61-1
p. cm – Green Integer 128
I. Title II. Series

Green Integer books are published for Douglas Messerli
Printed in the United States on acid-free paper.

for My DC Friends

They thought they wanted our God,
but what they really needed was an expert.

Contents

SUICIDE: starve

SALVATION: test

ABSOLUTE: equals

SUICIDE: starve

A kiss on the black cheek release.
Draw in deep to the filtered see.
It can't simply be smoked out or rained upon
paper. The improbable act, acts out of, stop. Fear.
Sought for another, or one, this.
Time down as it t comes slowly.
That which relates over-searched and stretched.
Your want here.
Leg extend to your stand before.
Death eats its own fill.
A kept from, and craving unknown.
Anticipated. Meditated. And uncertain.
But there, yes. Yes deep down the core.
A world on hold. Life suspended in mid-intake.
Feel the feel think again, not to finish
the finish. You know, you knew.
Forget the how in instinct home.
A call to arms. Yours.
If the hammer feels right.
Knee touch, kneel night.
Still, sort of sick.

OBJECT: relation

Getting a lost in to get at. Here
we're divided, fractured and hopeful not.
An eager ear so clear and willing
to uncover what stays between -
me and my lover. Take fucking cover,
wrap us up. This shake must be for you.
The broken few and forgotten.
Trapped & turning -
those lies ingested not swallowed.
Spit it up. Puke your stinking world, inherited
    disowned
sabotaged, bated & twisted. Your sink,
your head – flush it out,
not long before you're dead.

MIDDLE: excluded

Plain said and said so. Page down tuesday.

Oil wells and green field splinters, this year.

Old world poetry and the wasted paper leans upon
the in us.

Dance rapid and tight, enough to notice and not
care.

But to do and get done, already spent and not
providing.

Your pension is our poison. Flowers & bombs at
thank you.

Ten performances & awards, medals, honor – your
substance, abuse.

We are grafted, held, and fought. Precious and few,
on the mend -

torn, tattered, and made to mold. This rising retro-
action

upon the spin, uneven, clean & shaven.

This is dirty and obscene. A sight of laser light.

Pour that man a beer, shake the top down. Yo
mother fucker, new order hope.

KNOWLEDGE: cure

Know the thing and stand so. Mis-alighted and how.
This world numbered in name. The show and cable
   flip.
Allow me a long delicious pee and I could live on
   your lunches.
Our us imparted, transmitted, broken gospel learning
   faith.
Cathode eyes, screen blink. Paper bounce.
This meditated leisure sure is keeping me busy.
Take a class, fight a war. This cause is for you.
Stay, divided. The whole is best taken in part.
By the rampart's red glare you dare to exercise
   exclusion.
Fusion, re-combination, spliced genes, field report,
   remote,
press-conference, executive summary, year-end
fiscal statistics, real gross national product, third
   world
debt, leveraged buy-outs, small business options,
   padded books, personal

disposable income, lost our lease close-out sale,
limited time surrogate offer. Real large bodacious
   Christian revival.

Stop. Refrain. Let's all sing. Get ready. Come on
   everybody.
I was empty. Now I'm full. Yes, I was empty. Now I'm
   full.
Yes, so very very empty. Now so very very full. Slow.
   Repeat.
Fade.

ADVOCATE: don't wear black

My muse these days is a lit spoon. Impossible
morning blindness. Cream.
I want to scrape your insides out, add butter, add salt,
pull your poles and maybe
paralyze your Polaroids. Expose your snap shot stops
of this life.
Dried time. Only dried time dear. Your make-up
make believe, mold pressed vision.
The mundane fission of coming between. Coming
between yourself, these sheets.
Like going North to get South. Or running to the
East to fill up your West. Quest on
my hero. Lance me a dragon. Slay me a wizard.

How far out can you go to get in? Go on, try out.
Tire out. The little train that could
had a secret about knowing the right track. They
never tell you that.

Screw it. I just want to razor cut this rope wound
round your neck, sorry.

Sorry for the facts. Sorry for the fate. Sorry the way
the cards got dealt.

So, no real big deal. We are we – used to it. Welcome
to us.

Post-hype, post-post generation. Here we are post-out
looking to get back in.

The out-post generation – raised on division.
Schooled in revision.

A multi-media blitz of fractured mind. Sampled and
re-recorded.

We'll re-write the inside out.

DIZZY: morality

I said yo flip flop - welcome to top world.
This spinning excuse for society is yours.
Hand thread the hang time.
Wound tight and pulled fast.
The gun chases its own reason – street laid.
Wasted alley logic. Backed out and busted.
Say dude this is deal world – bagged and sold,
main lined out. Said make your own here.
This is a guilt free zone.

NOSTALGIA: report

A line that comes undone. Here honey your gun.
So sweet, so soft, so stiff. You're malleable in form.
I ask for butter but will accept lead. Take head.
Your sex excites my mind. Your cheese runs my dog.
For you a thought must be inside out. An act – a
   divine
scream. Your center hot and melting rage.
I know thinly concealed – welcome to your world.
Now February, think of snow even if your not.
Try to cover in white, recover the not lost. I slip,
hold tight to this shoot.

There are tears in my body. Tears in you.
Tears in your lake. Tears in the world.
Tears on the take. Tears all over and really not a single

drop. Know what I mean? The feel has fell from the
inside.

There stays the shell — take aim and launch. A site-
on.

Your cross hairs in my mouth. My weapon at your
brain.

This kind act so.

WORD STUPID: terminal

A calm quietly undone. Like you in the morning, in
    half recall, half disbelief.
This chain smoked dream, drug induced wonder, mind
    produced wander. Come.
You soul spoke your crazy energy high, dissolved into
    breath, and made it there.
Sorry, I've got a head full. Like the only sane response
    to this world *is* madness.
Your mother doesn't even know your name. You call
    me, you there — I say see.
This pendulum balance upon the precipice tip. Let's
    call the waiter, order steaks.
No this isn't the old world lyric and I am not a liar, so
    you satyr
stare, mural run, colosseum feast, chariot drive, and to-
ga wash our this.
It costs and you may choose to pay up — to get in the
    game, be a player,
be on the A team, be in the loop, get your say in, be a
    policy maker,
decision maker, earth shaker, one of the doers, one of
    the empowered, a real lifer.

Oh just stop. I can't take your cathode cubicle logic
   anymore.
So precise, so divided, so unoriginal. Forget seeing
   the forest dude.
You paper burn the chase. Spirit lock on plastic – sun
   kill
in designer tan. I can't say this pretty. I can't.

VAMPIRE: rape

So quick stabs into the wanting. In guise of true
    concern for another. Kill.
Your lack of look is all I see. You hand hold my neck,
    vanity stare my why.
When asked and made to speak, I bleed. You suck the
    day out of me. Night on
to your lack of star darkness. To take any other is
    crime.

Your ploy is grave plot absurd. Game speak this
    flowering imagery upon my tomb.
You debauch my soul, separating action from actions.
    Get it? Hope
you've had a real good. Decry the vile lack for other
    hid in mock empathy care. You
war me to death. Spike it. Pass me the bullet please.

SILENCE: bleed

For the cost and lack of smooth stroke, an ear. You
  chose to do my let.
A backhand across a slap, this hair pull – this rough
  fuck. And still
you cannot, no not touch this me. You are rope-
  world twisted.
A knot knocking this instance out. Go. Go
  grapepick, clover-
search, rainbow-watch away. You, a sunset on a never.
This, a cross passion, a bear, a poison allowance, an
  easy pill. You see?
An act of reverse control – a spin upon a stance, a
  self-induced
thorn. All in the place of. Place of ear-space. A
  listen, a look.
I'll take a forgive me on the rocks please. This is
  straight up.
Take your acid washed world. Meltdown.

SOCIAL ROMANTICISM: dropdead

Welcome to the days of longer morning. You take
  this – an easy
back rub to get your flow connect. This thinks,
  wanders in your wild.
Maybe its a place to hide. Cave spent – an
  underground dark and there.
Sometimes the most important thing to do *is* to write
  a poem. Fuck.
I can theorize your world away, produce ills and
  swords: Rocks and garden.
In a single word you were there. In two words, real
  big.
Here's the difference. Men may want to embrace the
  world, wide armed spread,
because they can. Flowers and soul, lead and guns:
  Control. Women, their legs.
You see, this reduction, the way the structure stalls.
  Arms cross becoming heart bombs.
A huge stop is this mind death. Some make it like it
  that way.
Trapped by a block, a cold from the inside. This is
  not choice, chance.

When the difference in priviledge is an x or y, the
    change is
single variable obvious, easy. Why is the difference in
    denim.
We all wear jeans. Let's rough ride a fix.

COMMUNAL: alienation

My days have numbers. A pot of coffee and a poem,
  you there, me.
This fate we desire, divides, overcomes the exclusion
  out. Push.
I this, me talk, is a leftover on the run. I faint see,
  color colors.
This is hand wrapped – a conversation with fingers,
  slow and smooth,
even. A single malt or take this take me. In, a
  hypnotic,
inclusion swallowed. A line bend, a straight steer to
  formula.
For the price of a few integers, I know I can count on
  you.
Let's galaxy flip, and countdown – space stride
  between planes. We
can free fall thought tumble, zero G body dock, mind
  orbit
through layers of what. I know our need. A mid-flight
  minor
course correction generation. Breathing fumes and
  exhausted.

This is a hand hold. A system check. Provisions
    packed,
we are fueled, space kid ready. This now then. This
push past the home pad and frontier grasp our us at
goodbye speed. An escape generation
accelerating our necessary. This is liftoff. Velocity
    out.

INVENTORY: echo

Where collisions collide and the upon of this dies. Your
　　bloomers knicker down.
He wrote ninety pages every night just so he could
　　remember to forget.
Self lies in the past – arm grasp that wrap around.
　　Look, I
don't want you to face history but that is where you
　　begin. Adapt
to the you you become, then talk the story of my
　　people and let.
I've got to go to the mountains on this one. If it were
　　only colonial
I would raise tobacco, talk politics and revolution,
　　debate old country
philosophy, install new government, and cotton to your
　　notions of freedom.
Well fed upon the subjugation of others. What changes
　　changes the doom
of a destiny you may well repeat. Knowledge at your
　　back is not always
gentle or kind. Key upon the maternal raise. Look hard
　　at the patriarch.
Sometimes we're screwed from the start.

ANIMAL: hiatus

If this is solely an exercise in deprivation, then I
   confess you win.
I wake from no sleep street smart and want to fall
   into full music and scum.
The lack of time has made me stupid – wrath has me
   soul numb.
I used to think bullets, pills, high windows, bridges,
   tracks, wrists,
water, gas (both kinds), cooking, cars, and rope but
   never that it would be
simply you. I lice shower alone in my holocaust
   room, feel your scorned
indignation crossing anger into lack of consequence
   resentful punishment.
Take a break. Both bones and marrow eventually rot
   or support this dying life.
The earth gives way to mother. If in the natural order
   of things you evolve, some
shit will say you're just a write off. A reduction of
   belief equals a lack of truth.
If it feels right, sometimes it simply just feels right.
   Gut know the furry reaction thus.

ESTRANGED: kin

Twisted mesh of mangled wreck, you are black silk
    and gunboat boots.
Two kids and a car, two lines and nothing said. So I
    fall back
upon your habitat. This jungle leaves my mind in
    your vine.
This is our playground. Disneyland. Graceland.
    Vineland. Drink in.
For the single cost of admission you can fly to the
    moon, kiss the earth
goodbye.

Face down: Blood pool. I hide my stash, my jeans.
    You slash your sash.
This is ropeworld: Violent, twisted, and calm. Buy
    me another drink.
Tip over my yes. Fold my face, softly. Oh, beauty:
    Justice.

Thank you for taking the time to string me out.
  Along our heritage
I've come to know home: Grafted, sediment, and
  kind. I shake
your hands, you kiss my cheek. A small
  admonishment demonstrates care.

For this a life becomes paper, nothing more. Home
  and harm.
Beautiful meals, broken dishes. I adopt a straight
  line.
Here we are placid: Glass, turbulent, deep. Tide
  upon the sand. Bound.
Breaking to speak, learning to scream.

PERIPHERAL: next
        for Joe

Subjugated and kind, I cannot. This, ends
end in the noise of. Our us torn before tatter.
We eat this world, hungry half alive, never full and
    overfed.
My call a surprise. Who cares and shatters the why.

These quiet shouts of inside out. Hello, go away –
    take back your nothing.
It is a play, a pastime last resort, digging the green
    beans and dirt.
Put on a record, I'll strip to your spin. I'll skip to your
    beat.

Early years and frost. Always the standing of
    everybody's outside in. Birthright.
We are refused and denied – blocked up and
    controlled. A cap upon the
core there. My voice cracks the tears of your stupid
    nod.
I weigh the playdown this dead and numbing game
    and a bit short of make.

I call far ahead and touch your there hand. I'll pocket
     grasp
your coin purse and step back knowing you'll never.

The sun sets in the color of my head. A completed
desperation and laughing sound track. Please take a
     number, I'll call.
This fruitstand world: This shelf with the lid on.

DISCORD: smoke

The eyes become electric glass. You flicker your sex
   walk, hit me with a line.
We're talking dirty and tight, thinking challenge
   poverty and clay.
Formica sound boards have gotten me high strung
   and I've been known to
fall in love with several variations of fear. Come leg
   stretch your way here babe.

For our next act we require a finger nail file. Crossed
   up and confused, let's empty
our hand searching. It is morning in your hair –
   twisted and numb. Let's
shampoo our breakfast, fry some whys, crack the
   toast, butter
the wheat. I'll meet you in the next field of pain.

How much distance can be said. Take head. Cross
   sex me with your breasts,
thighs, forearms, hips, cock, belly, back, cunt, neck,
   eyes,
lips, finger tips, nose, tongue, tits, calves, wrists,
   ankles,
smiles, ears, sides, curves, shoulders, and nerves.
   Yeah.

O.K. You're here. I meet you at the end of shout, just
   before reaching's out.
We stay over-stimulated, mutilated, and secure, a
   shout too far
at what's shouting back. I hear you're here, circuit
   over load.
Someone flip the switch. I'll see you all in the dark.

PROGRESSION: cigarette
          for Jim Pegg

I dreamed I ran out of paper. You had to platform
    jump to your back, applause.
When distance in flight equals the time spent
    learning to leap, I'll call
you brother, sister, mother, wise one, lover, friend,
    one
of the chosen, romantic, confused, true, guiltless,
    tough,
ready, paid up, learned, spontaneous, righteous,
    outrageous,
uncontrollable, smart, beautiful, sexy, and offer to
    buy
you a drink. O.K. So I know your want, don't be
    jealous.
The gift said is gift regardless of giver. Got it?

So we went out looking for this big it. Caught wind.
  Traces.
This bear too big for one to bring down, but only one
  must.
Tonight I lace up my snow boots, sand walk into
  palm night,
follow deserts to beaches, plant a little, harvest a little,
  take back
fruits, gather some sky. Don't ask, receive – and there
two feet. Prints: Only prints.

ETHIC: heal
    for Barb II

Today we take score: Two saved, one lost, three
    together, one apart.
Another not spoken of and gone, one that was saved,
    lost. One lost,
now saved, making another to add to total six. This
    number crunch.
So I figured the length of the project equals the time
spent working on it. The soul. A thought out and
    running wild.
How the wheels tend to spin on their own and I
    sawdust back away.
This apprentice world, viper-eyed: The cobbled
    heart. Out
spoken, a play in slow motion train wreck left deep
    sea wishing
and how the bubbles burst the brain. Welcome to
    your life line
tethered spine. You novice watch, interfere with mud.
A step up into a step into away and dangerous. They
    watch.

A paranoid frenzy, incomprehensible to outside
   wonder.
Let the watch, watch. Hand over the hand bound.
This is a manual curse, roll up your sleeves. Hammer.

ASSIMILATE: inure

I wake up polluted. Your three brands of stupidity
   afloat in my veins: Hate, curse
and the spell strands the cat. Brew on — infusion adds
   speed to this mix.
If it were a shorter subject, I would use less words.
   Maybe, violent.
Like how when a bullet is seen as kind. Word order
   dogs chance.
This intention on a leash, lead on — of course you
stay
   collared,
pulling the choke, tension on a line taut. Old
   teachers, lost
leaders, a sales come-on. Don't buy in, it kills.

You spider weave a fine between hanging on and
   gone. Architecture.
A design and shape to stick your head in. Heart on its
   own.

First place first, when intrusion becomes desperate and necessary,

clothes are optional. A means of keeping the skin on - bare boned.

We skull watch. Black leather eye socket the too much. Seen not felt.

A defense gone astray, away. A way of life, no. Survival.

LANGUAGE: stump

These words so foreign and sure. The where from not
   here, so sorry.
So take - this all in. Your nerves on drugs, body
   stung. Hand
out, steady and shaken. This yes for you. Forget the
   retro-action,
thruster boost. I'll meet you in that space. Crazy and
   fucked up.

I want to cross every "t" with you. Wake up the shake
   up and see.
Will I you remember the morning. A light shining
   through.
Purpose, the repose on stilts. I clown watch, you
   laugh.
I love you, forget it. Words to the tender other. Dress
   black and bleed.
Tie optional. We have a request from their office.
   Memo this it, babe.

Words at first divide. No, at last divide. No, are cause
   of and cure.
No, words make the me us whole. After division.
   You two, me
one. No won. No too. Complicate the page. Tear
   your tear out.

This manila folder. This hurried rush. Slow. File.
   Exercise your coffee.
This thing becomes self. Propelled. You know, it sure
   is a good thing you look
good. Let's fill this ashtray up. Garden. Weed your
   whys on seed. Plant.
Raise a major addiction. Get up your get up. Word
   write far far away.

Hold tightly near the head. Close cover before
   striking. Best results.

HERITAGE: finish
for Mallarmé there

I cross count blank pages. Exhaustion equals the end
    of book - take bets.
The odds are on a one horse race. Erase the wire, crap
    out,
I'll throw down. Dice gamble their loss. God and
    universe are one.
Annul, one half, yes. This new nation: In we, we
    trust.
Finger pick your tofu away. Eat gravy, spill seeds.
    Oh.
The land of liberty, torches your freedom. Change
    name.
An island off the coast. Bean sprout and feed the
    world.
Connect the cable and deep dish your satellite. Now,
    here,
photo shop your this wire. Correspondents on,
    prompter fed.
At the sound of the beep: Slow speak your name,
number, and time of call.

INCARNATION: bare

There is no it there being smoked to the core. Empty
    rooms and hope: Left.
Stranded on the edge of strategy, you are the only and
    forget once again comes to mind.
We need longer lines, shop the stand past rotted fruit
    and feast.
Time the clock and say more empty full words:
    Meaning is remembrance.
At the point where you teach the heavy said – full im
    pact and loss not being.
Minutes become nightmares. A horse ridden, put
    away wet, appetite.
This craved, soul spoke and sure. Music for the gone
    world, haunted.
What you could not recover becomes grave. A last
    say, said.
This a letting go of the foregone, conclude and begin,
    speaking a swirl and then.
Care can only, the cut, sharpen up. Stand back full
    ahead. Write the writing out.
You know what you're doing – confirmation this
    accord, world rope. In the event

of an emergency, tell everyone you know to freeze!
  Dry ice equals smoke.
Count the lines and sudden the know. Read slow and
  wound tight. This exercise
in exclusion, inclusion of too much. Self aware.
  Referential. You there.

BORROW: psychopath

O.K. I am method acting. Tenor sax. Blowing five to
the – beat it.

Sometimes it is too easy. Work out the say there and
fess up dude. Wild

and stray the strand of this abandon. You will know
tomorrow, steady hand.

You seem to tend to the loss and in between, the gap.
Built to explode

and the wire connects stick to back. Ignore, leave the
under skin.

You sir, are out of order. How to speak the not there,
trace and race.

Write small and sure. Clarity in brief short shouts at
the coming out.

Sister, yo. What that you be wear'in? Them there say
yeah.

EXTINCT: elegant

When they are those times – nothing read matters.
    Things written blow
with want of grace to their own insignificance: Here
    said thus demise.
Story book in your fable eyes – reap grim an apple's
    hold. Music claims
its need to speak and having lack of say fades, too.
    Longing, lodging
the craving to articulate squarely upon this wreck of
    one.
Sorry, I think I can't explain this sudden lack of
    moon, or if only
everyone else had it too, the foreign. Hand shake the
    enemy hold.
There really isn't any fear. Requiem equals
    celebration, but for one.
Call my carriage, feed well the horse. All is ash, soil
    to the dirt,
heap my try holy upon the sullen and the few. Write
    out
spent what the hand held now holds you. Go.

INDICTMENT: challenge

I bed to your traces. A smell upon my tongue
   wondering at the words.
Having seen the show you pack bag and go. This
   brief case, carry your weight.
If I could issue an executive decree, it would be, drop
   dead. Thump.
And yes, I say that with love. Having power to give
   world orders, you
choose what let to do. A cheap run from the better
   known. Enough.
O.K. so confusion. The time it takes to look words
   up— that I understand.
This lost in swirl strewn with vine is a choke hold ripe
   and picking ready.
You're dyslexic in truth. Got the down side up.
   Goose kill, get up.

SHIFT: change

Count up to the counting down – tie up the tapping
    down. Brilliance is
that blaze by, the passing through making light in the
    dark. Horse laugh
at the brain fry barbecue. But I must admit, since I've
    learned to cook, I sure
do eat better. I take double servings and side order
    death. Question: Is love
ground? Is love meaning? Is love there? Is love
    hope? Is love real? Is love il -
lusion? Is love pleasure? Is love loss? Is love just
    concept? Word only, is
love, love and why. We lean upon the learned to take
    form from understanding.
Stand on upon the upright there, righteous and
    impassible upon your rock
hold of the knowledge and wisdom there. Light up
    the smoked down.
Mystical is only the mist. A fog around what is
    missed, a refuse to cut.
On the day of my heart attack, I knew I had let guards
    down. Hope there.
A late round maybe come back. Somewhere I'm a
    head on points.

55

REVENGE: band

Due to the complete lack of inspiration, learn to talk
    this in shorter lines.
A pre-dawn wake up leaves me lack of sun cold. State
    the obvious and key
on the reverse of this spin. I don't know yet, do you?
    Fill the form with
the extra baggage you've managed to luggage around,
    train stop.
Conduct the next symphony in your head and just
    try to find an orchestra
that will play that fire. Go make the mythology of
    place justify being stuck.
Other world call: Should have turned on my
    machine. Indulge this dear
reader, the signs upon you. Having said he had
    nothing else to say
he managed to talk on for over forty years more,
    dumb euthanasialess
mother-fucker. Turn the machine off, turn the
    machine on. Turn
one page left blank. Write the nightmare with found
    wood, build

home from possibly thousands of wants. Bury the
   line in the sand.
Force out, face in, call your own tune. Pay the piper
   with credit notes,
lose the poetry voice and answer the press. Review
   this in hindsight.
The critic knows no blood and you've gone and asked
   him to the ball.
Well, blow me over, dance that devil.

NUANCE: absence

A sickness at the pit of this. (I think). Frantic search
for the sympathetic other.

Know you to find me, write large. Bold print shouts
like how

do you survive? Easy seen from the outside in, not
me? Intense

intensity searching closer on looks back. Too short
sentences. Distrust

the rightly so of language. If I were to repeat myself
would you.

Empty Bach of his number – self referential – equals
end.

We talk of the final, make notes and learn keys. We
do know what we need.

The weight of the thing folds tired face down. Dog
eared and there.

A pack a day, wolf's bane and close out. There's no
easy way

to end this is to start, this. But that's been said
before, feel now.

Read each sentence again, again. Slowly.

OVERLOAD: stifle

You come through the door and hit me with several
    layers of your boredom. Say,
act me a cure, entertain my life away. Honey, no.
    Sprout your own brand of weed.
Killer or gardener. Any of the several varieties in your
    head feed, flower please.

See, I live in this valley of spoon where forks divide
    everyday. Choice,
a forestall of peace and coercion is another name for
    the current government. I
must lead on upon the follow that is just slightly
    ahead of this me regime. Hurry up
to the next polls, don't keep word makers waiting.
    Grow past world faker, lend
hand hang complaint. Raise drink before wine sours
    in this near ear glass.

So I confess to your lack of malice. Understand your
  narrative of care.
This excess breath takes, doesn't lend life more. I
  flying in an already overly
pressurized cabin. Cut the flow, someone may strike
  a match.

NATURAL: end
    for S.S.N

Yes, that it picks up steam – a momentum carrying us
    through: And passion.
Or the lack, that will break us. "Challenge the *people*
    to start a revolution."
Slide beyond the step where emotion must come in,
    this is antenna race.
If the game goes into overtime, we will be ready.
    Silent, sure, and full.
There's a lot to fuck you up. Treated, evaluated,
    judged. Don't
give in. Hold, rest upon this head. Heart out larger
    meals, taste.
The public is universal and there sometimes denied,
    political and subjective.
Under the glass and examined for kindness and
    decency – this mind numbing
madness when it all seems so obvious though tough.
    Strength out.
Obligations have me down, bound to want and
    correct. Speak says
about nothing and being. Passion is born and leaves
    open wound.

Rejection is only the not yet comprehensible but
inevitable: Thrust.

We meet in the basic, the elemental human and wait,
needs to change.

The conditions of our if is. Disappears with tolerance
and involved.

Long the wait. Lifted. World gives. Out.

WOUND: mate

This vessel head pops in its own excursion. A vain
    attempt to carry
the cargo to your port: Heart out. A dry dock in land
    lock lack of blood.
One big dry fuck pump on. All of us are sailors with
    our own
flags to fly. You, honey though are the pirate of this
    soul. Ship on -
rough seas have tossed my thought, skin stink, my
    drink. This foam
is madness not the frosty head kind, but with sea legs
    and sure.
I've brain licked every image I could to navigate to
    your stars,
but still the first mate rock steers toward wreck. Coast
    on your course,
good luck to the kiss off natives. There's mutiny on
    the land in take over
arrogance supreme. Captain over board. That
    mother fucker
sure could sail.

FEMININE: blaze

I walk out slowly to the end of tobacco, feel the chair
  sink below me.
The nerves calm finally to the point of death: Don't
  fire. Slowly, slowly.
Still this assured resolve – solve the puzzle. Last
  pieces in place: Corpse rot.
I don't want to take this to the end of light, delight in
  closing: Eye shut.
Le verbe ne dit rien. Can't. Act. Fell the touch of my
  last cigarette, last meal.
Light up and care: Dare. Yes, it is too all too much.
  In sections read.
Add the spice of wet hair. Shampoo happy days.
  Daytime lies.
It keeps it all spinning. Home make me home. Clean
  out the half eaten pot.
This record scratched, itch and bleed for all to see:
  Learn. Just a record.

Phone talk transatlantic truths, make the space for.
   Roll over.
Thank you for being the fire. This setting son glows
   red. You
a rising moon. Choose. Exhausted, or sleep. This
   brave act so.

HUNGER: poison

In my quest to feed and be fed some hideous truth
    sinks in. Face off.
The mask of meal consumes your feast. Bloated
    corpse walking night.
I craved sustenance for some wisdom or what I could
    give back. Pass gravy,
the fat, dripping juice for your dress taken from this
    cooking meat. Your recipe,
add salt to whatever's open. Read, to cure. Preserve
    only yourself by sealing
the rest off. Wax on, honey. Some claim the want is
    painful. Hell. I'd rather
fast alone with chance than follow like you and eat
    this world.

SALVATION: test

Is it on Earth? Reached.
My piano monks out to this lived played touch.
The wreck of us here. Religion does equal out.
Interchangeable with each other.
The anguish of being: Is Alone. A wish,
I go through. Human divine.
Help yourself, to our hour here.
Burnt ends crisp, the waiting
us naive and analysis, an amazing error.
Worship in the trees, spirit speak -
a place warm and strong leaves
several changes of mind: Food, home.
That's all - we can hope, for a simple peace.
You watch, this listen -
the way the heat builds.
Pick out the left overs. Credible, sure.

ORDAIN: cost

First, throw out all notions of sin. Create or let that
   space at the end of skin.
I come back to count the empty bottles. take stock,
   flip open want.
Context, the container of necessity. Form, simply the
   action of the shake. And
content, the you to do. A fill up, threatening the
   breadth of this wide.

I don't want it shorter, just better. Like how I already
   feel the push away.
A close come. Very near and dear. But ultimately the
   thing said, divides.
Or rather, pushes the show and you to stage, but can't
   perform. You will
refuse to be content as audience. The figures front
   the fire: Priest burn.
Turn. Look.

SENTIMENT: noise

Take a stretch across this bared breast. A physical
motion to release snap. You shut, cut up paper rock.
A desire you should have remembered but never.
    Wasn't there.
T.V. ad. Glowing gems forgot the water. Trust this.
It is sunrise in your arms. We walk on your cool
    forested beach.
I take you mountain walking. You fix me breakfast
    bed.
I buy you fireplace flower gifts. You call me secret
    names. I forget
other other's and accompanying want. You tell your
    friends.
I speak secret words. You tell magic charms. I speak
    louder
shouts. You invoke dark witches. I scream. You spell.
I don't understand. You do. Stop.

We walk by fresh laundry smells. Lunch time milk
    money.
This safe room sometimes scary at night - the sounds
    come in.

Our legacy places are empty full, so we speak the
   stuffing out.
More volume to quiet down, a try to reach around.
   Take -
this hand, out. Bleeding too.

SLEEP: song

Stunned and shimmied I walk to your turbulent
   world. A wake
incensed and draped in colors of lead. Your state
   states my case,
causes a full explosion in this early morning ambush
   air.
No, how could I be ready prepared for a tarpaper
   necklace. I'll
wave seeya from my moon glide, I'll throw kisses
   from my beamride.

Let's cradle rock together. Sing sand – blanket cover
   – horse warmth.
There's a million stars behind those lids, and no rea
   son to keep your face in a jar.
I've sheep counted notes on your pillow and pills in
   your hand.
I promise I'll be kid kind tonight. Each of us prone
   and tight.
Come on, let's stretch our horizon, fold dreamy space
   down our tired verticals.

TEMPORARY: exclusive
for Mary, Again

This how in you: A gift hold across an otherwise
    divide, take.

Intake, cool smoke into your breath speak to believe
    and its at.

Easier than your before thought. Think and spin,
    slap face.

Fuse meld your con-mold then insert toe-hold plastic
    care, someone.

This ambivalence is your ally, your prey, your quarry.
    Dig.

Cut throat and rocks. I wanted your what's there,
    settle for stalls.

I go to war every morning. You battle my day. Fuck
    you, thank you.

Keep the middle in and survive on besides. Torpedo
    this lettuce

for working too hard. Sorry, stay. Put on your day
    wall.

SIMULACRUM: balance

When the world comes back, my next cigarette and
    pepsi. Head clear,
time warp day trip stop becomes a clearing of
    Romantic field. An epic inferno Eden.
Such is our this. I want your was, fuzzy and smooth -
    tickle my razor.
Let's sleep in layers of hell. I can't get warm — word
    frozen, divided.
Every question answered. Every riddle stupid -
    knowledge dead. Wisdom worried & old.
This is where I me find you, there dear. So tenderly
    twisted - So brutally resisted. I rest
your confusion in my me song. You sing clear noted
    refrains. Scream resigned harmony.
This double duo, twinned life without other. Egg
    split fusion is.
I want to rock this world away. Romantic longing,
    annihilation care.
We flower pick our choices and drink deep our
    poison. Refuse say, our voices.

Yes I am already thinking of tomorrow. A next,
  hopefully more. An again

beginning each row, each wave. Straining back
  muscles, full arms. Call me

other names than myself knows and I'll respond to
  your there core. Building shell.

We step back into a growing an, slice chop retreat into
  an already.

I want to cave lick the future. You fire make home.

VISCERAL: meat
         for Barb

To look in to stand what looks out, Ouch. How the
    hurt equals thrust, trust.

The pill poison plus two, minus one. Like, I thought
    I've said that before.

You must know, on automatic. The pilot of this craft
    asleep and boring.

Honing in on your instinct, intact, behind cages and
    their faulting, preservation.

The thing said and lost in its keeping, a perfection
    within mold, slim and reserve.

Take aim against this pre-dawn. Drawn to no other
    and its next, I see you there.

Stranded, cold and waiting. This is curly and
    circuitous – sitting against a setting out.

So we take will. Not speak of the not spoken is
    endured, etched and reassured.

A whim on a walk, a freak on a stick. Wear other
    clothes than the horse assumes.

We set against a setting out. A dissolve into this scene
    and order cream and fudge.

Take waiters and their cues while we live in ice world,
   worried sick and still

ringing between the waits and where the car drove up
   to drop off this easy ride.

We were forced to thumb stick, side wait, and con
   template several brands of sky.

You look to define intrusion with a nod, with a word:
   Wooden, Shielded, Branded.

MANIC: dance

Dig beat blank drop good. Pounding around. Bass
    your way
to this lick. Slow fast resurrect timber time equate
    new.
Word salad jumble fry your best on. Seen seen would
    if at better but.
Floppy found book shelf down. O.K. O.K. run run
    car board town.

Sometimes a yes is a better but. Introduce the band.
    Take bow.
A cut in maybe may in. Let's call the square, a square.
    Waltz would
cast an otherwise divide. Skirt this hoop, jump.

OVERT: evidence

Like clearing the throat. A reverse voice, say again -
   affirm that the.
In the middle, both ends can be seen clearly, you
   knew that. The
furthest from becomes a safe place there. The
   majority stays bunched. To
one extreme is the other. The my place. I lay low to
   fly, far out
to find home. In the flow the stream carries its own
   weight.
Don't wait up. A step in the place of same spot,
   possible. Yes.

ETHEREAL: ground

This begins on the run. A complete and sudden lack
of time, curious. Face away.

Early – still ours, morning shy. Experience falls the
begin with so much want of here.

Page back to the start of there, there the loss. Calls
call the scream between.

I dream this to you, the after flow of a life lived. Pass
a double grace please.

I've seen your starry eyed face down side. Load up on
glue, find what sticks.

Intensity fill the space full this loss of muscle will and
the accompanying snap.

Written well with found thought, think it out again to
recover the bury.

Say the say said for new ears and rearrange the stones.
Strand the act by

acting the part of deliverer, save some cream for the
top. It is too easy to give

out. I need some secret: Strength. To affirm the
denial twist the switch in

your head and see through the refuse. Fuse full the
meld of confuse with

presence behind the absence hid, come back. Touch
and its earth -

beautiful brown warm sound. Rank your goodbyes
by measuring hellos.

Hero be, roll the mud and form clay with spoon
fingers. Eat deep and stay.

MANUAL: stock

If in the space of, you can breathe. Wind will become
   and your run on.
Take stock, day order other nexts and walk away
   towards similar undone.
Instructions, envious of their perception and true lack
   of said, sure.
This laid out, seemingly plain. Simple the nod with
   in the core hold.
And yet, a definite certain lack of. A must trust in
   your face and curious,
vacuous the solid of geometry and other meters.
   Measure
the number of rooms times the time of stay and allow
   the guests
to order softer towels, papers, full splits, half stops,
   other parties,
and chase away the lost. All this, but for one night.
   No, decisions
can't be made and fully understood under this
   influence, kid nap,
suggest, or coerce of there. Not yet, but nearly the
   next to.

So, we drive faster, test the brakes, crave higher
   octane, two wheel

the curves, run the lights, say stupid backseat stuff,
   tape over

the mirrors, turn out the lights, polish the chrome,
   and push the metal.

But all the while look out for cops. This makes sense?
   No, babe.

Touch down, short order flight, pull up the gear and
   foam the runway.

This is system check. Engage. Phones will not do,
   rage on.

JUSTIFY: resolve

We come to the beginning and call it loss. Desperate
    and certain what
the mind made up you take as rock. Go cliff walk,
    climb about ledges,
slippery moss and peaks – body tired, shaking hold.
    Shiver you ice
dry with time and longer whys. Pour this down the
    pipes of absolute yes.

There is no track back. Buy longer fishing poles and
    learn to plant. You can't
but help to can. Every each inside your red beat.
    Pound out
the weight with your rhythm lift. O.K. sure you get
    the drift of this rift.
The pretty sleeps ugly, wakes to head dresses and
    bows. Try on.

CONSPICUOUS: strand

Cup the ear and order another – smoke said. Your
   next love hump, figure sure.
Chair out to the end of sky, reply requested at the
   when. So just
pressure this to the absence and the wait – feed on
   and send. I
think you said meet me there. There's too many
   words to say the simple.
I know you feel the wait and endure past dear, but
   what I need is a
nap on the run, a thank you on the take. Hello:
   Gone blonds. The magic
fades at the announce of this. This contradiction like,
   press release.
You ever try that? Button down your button up, zip
   on bye. When
urinals smell like perfume, you're either in the wrong
   place or in trouble.

Flush out with a smile, an inside joke. Be one of the
    boys, learn

the rules and make the breaks, clear. I cigar salute the
    old days, like

how it was so easy then. Know that illusion and
    rough up, map to come.

The blow up, the blow out – some of you just have
    got to go. For me,

I'll finger pick through the remains. Fine like friends
    that follow the fall out.

RE-VISION: notes
            for Jim, Charlie

The easy comes in too easy. These notes still ringing
    in my ear, between

two beats. Now I know double song. Yes, A. If only
    it were, simple other.

A vaulted arch, a chair where only one could sit. This
    on the take.

I know, you know. A double entendre giving life,
    taking life.

Abort the lack of courage, seal safe within. I don't
    want

to talk of phoenix, choose the desert for its lack of
    what I bring.

Thirst, yes to tired eyes, straining body – water rites.

A baptismal of simple fire, flame on. This form
    lacking. Lacking

you to fill, split the softer voice. I don't deserve
    room.

Crash here upon my carpet, where you are. I repeat,

refrain from. A ringing, in tense quiet. Click upon
    the, the.

Has it ever been said before? Liberal at its loss. This
    ground
shakes the seed for more awake stronger bean. Drink
    —
please drink. Between two the intoxicate of the lucid
    want. I
need end not yet in blue or black or back or a head
    bobbing
in the wind. A wave upon the sea is sea, womb peace.
    When
one is another. Yes, when one is another, call is
    correct.
Three's: Plagal cadence, diminished seventh's
    complete,
the chord. Accord. That simple, sure.

ISOLATE: heal

O.K. so I admit to not knowing how to fill your
    blank page. Admit too,
I wouldn't want to — old notions and let's kill these:
    Ownership, possession,
jealousy, rage, anger, guilt, competition, and the salad
    served on bread.
You see, we come from the same garden, snake pass.
    Top dog under.
And suddenly one stops and says to you, "How the
    fuck you doin' dude."
And belief comes fleetingly back. 'Till you're on your
    own again."
Divide the world from yourself and you die. See.
    Separation equals contempt.
Hell, we're all the same. Say, "stop", say "hi". Keep it
    easy,
sure, short and forever. Forever, yes.

ADAPTIVE: connect

I start every morning with a prayer. End each night
   with a seduction. And in between protect.
I don't think this world can invent many more ways
   to keep you from feeling. Anything
becomes its own instant loss. Your cup flows waste
   water river to dying sea. Polluted want.
One big cesspool flush. You too easily toxic waste
   bury your half life soul and forget our natural
environment is the body. Learn growth through
   leaning trees, walk about the forest
in pine needle heaven, roll in the leaves and be
   pleased. Where leaves are organic and not
a see you later, maybe. There's just not time. Left or
   Right or write this world up.
Ticket your our own us course. Mind reach another
   vision even through black heart.
Let's stay in there pumping, dude. Do we talk of
   blood? C'est la guerre. When
only catastrophe induces response. Somehow we
   know it shouldn't be like this but don't

know what to do. Right? Well, I don't mean to seem
   earthy crunchy but I'm tired
of this earth crunch. It is us. First find someone and
   chew the fat as a start. Cut to the chase.
Like a friend of mine says, follow that instinct. The
   hard road is survival and more. Thrive.

GNOMIC: gnostic

In the day time lack of want you sister stare in
   dissolving moon. Waxing
the poetic floors again, measuring hate in cupfuls of
   sugar – there and not.
Here and gone, taken and flown from, pressed and
   molded apart, lucid and crazy,
crazy and absolutely lucid. Completely said and not
   yet even begun. Sick
and so healthy. Coughed up and divided together we
   look square necessity.
Flour becomes bread, bread becomes roses, roses be
   comes water,
water becomes thirst, thirst becomes river, river be
   comes wine,
wine becomes warmth, warmth becomes truth –
   truth becomes you.
Drink your eat up and wash down to sustain the
   incredulous. Look,
I don't need to make this overblown so let's get terse.

First, creativity knows no generation. Likewise,
   passion and the search. And also

throw gender the fuck out. Yes, biology is difference
   but humanity is same,

saves. Run down that division with the biggest
   fastest truck you can find.

Next, subjugation. I am sick of control, power, and
   greed. So, no more.

Say so and live it. Then the harder stuff, like nurture.
   It is in all our nature,

but too many hand outs leaves you broke, broken,
   empty, silent, no good.

Don't get me wrong, compassion, yes. Reach to your
   fellow and

love, love only. Never live through. O.K.? O.K., so
   poetry climbs

down the mountain — in life as should ought be. Di
   vision still is there.

The given and the given to. Take, help out.

ENIGMA: excuse

Any one of these could end it. Yes pain and hurt
   sometimes
equals joy and that's it. Time collapses, Earth bound
to the water each gives. Said so and see. If it were
only so simple as saying, "I'm sorry." Not enough to
oil change and lubricate the heart of this matter.
   Matters.
Only ink will do, an island of bikini clad hope –
   skimp
on the lack of. Sonnets and their truth held in pieces
   of
worn cloth. String the instrument, strum on. In
the lack of perfection I so suddenly once again
   become human.
Your lesson – taught and taut. Moon skips pages and
   black.

Rap to your own beat, speak sometimes Italian or
  other
foreign gods. The ground breaks open. Cracks fill
  the space
of nothing and said, "I love you, I do." Hair tonic
  and
spray your culture and its inherent loss directly into
  your head.
I meant to write straight, but slant. Here they leave
you alone, but watch. Don't bomb out. Sight on,
  automatic.

PLAGIARISM: scribe

Words can become windows out of through which
   you stare. Clean glass
flowing top down, like the stained of ancient
   cathedrals. Thicker
at the bottom, lighter the higher you go. Spiritually
   so this straining
metaphor trying to equal the poetic device that you
   are. So sue me.
This silly pain, pundit humor. Don't deny, don't
   confuse
fame and the defaming of yourself. Like some
   people's only goal
is to have their name in the dictionary. Reduction is
   lack of oxygen.

When you get down to it, repetition. Cycles answer
   why with another
question at the beginning of end. Seems clever and
   stupid.

An easy way out is to watch it come back. Your job,
    renewal

and maybe a little more spice in. They were too
    young to be so old.

They were too old to be so young. Twist around the
    walk

around of sides and disguises. Take cloth – wipe,
    again.

DIVINE: relativity

Excuse, forgive me. They want me to be brilliant
    again, shine on.

When the end of my head is fire, I'll coal lick your
    thought too.

Attention, attention. Half an hour left, that's all, get
    it in.

The clock speeds its own strike, hour down to lift off.

Space, and what you only can fill. Please, don't let
    me down.

Read and go on. Fill up y(our) our own empty blank.
    Hand shake

the, "don't change a word legacy." Forget spelling
    and see.

The world need at the end of ash. Think out and de
    fine the us.

Can you read this? Yes, add on please, I can, can't
    make it.

I think too much, love too much, call in the lawyers.

This is altitude out. Nose bleed, face distort a yes.

Cut this to save the our time, carry on, before us
    made.

No, it wasn't the easy out, hair clumps. Carry on,
    carry on. Please.

FOLKLORE: explanation

Wake up and paper read the world together. Your
    cause, and excuse why.
You cannot just coffee drink your way to nirvana and
    forget – abort your no.
This isn't the happy news hour to feed off your credit
    card disillusion. Break
your plastic hold of human life with blood, pump it.
    Feed on for your fellow.
The one there needs you.

Day care distractions make soup of the mind. Heart
    out of ground,
rhythm lack. The call of the buzz and feel of the spin
    – yes, you too.
One is prime, steak out the start. You begin first.
    Stage on, as an example,
he refused to throw the dog just a bone. Cast fish
    pearls. Net gains equal care.
Shine.

WIRED: logic

Most arguments get reduced to a single proposition. I
    believe this, you that.
Forget the feeling in between, and consequence is,
    "how do I go on."
Survival – the lack of compassion engulfed as a sound
    bite, chew on.
What gets often left out is who. Hold the hand
    steady and cut on.
Many levels of hope dissolve to instant instinct. Like:
    women love and want
to help men, but hate each other home. Win one for
    the home team. Or,
only men truly know how to share, bond, where the
    place they make is larger,
growing. Solace in the only each other. Isn't a
    wonder
that we're not all gay. Civil rights and argued wrongs
    – and the court
is stacked against our us. The robes we wear are
    androgynous.
Tie it up above the waste of our lost land – cross
    circuit the inbreed.

We must get above the body legislating the law in us.
  Think your way

to the heart that makes no sense. Incense stronger the
  anger of how.

We you *can* get there from here. Plug socket, light on.

TRANSITION: peace

Search hard the empty petal. We're washed
up and deserted, a generation in change. Dimes time
calls to other parties – shorter lines tangled
in their want of flower. Bake on when it's all.
Held in the head of, the in you, only on
several channels at once. Your job, sort out the say.
You can't possibly take it all in: Divided as survival.
No blame to the maid spinning the laundry.
Towel dry your night time care, order two.
Indulge the band for lack of stand and drink up.
Place one foot squarely in the in between. Balance,
your smile behind the arms, shoot your mouth.
I've got splinters in my teeth while we learn to love
space. Guess I've got time for the outer orbit.

MAN MADE: remembrance

Haunted by the trap of world, a wet wheel spun
   highway. We
ride on our coffee thoughts, unable to derange
   enough to make
sense of – slow traffic right, I want. Map lost, folded
   and creased,
but we're O.K. A drive-thru generation – aimless but
   sure.
We ghost town visit our old deserted places, one
   without. Remember
us there? A lost for nostalgia. Times better felt in
   retro – a loss of now.
When we are still here. Better feel, come touch my
   reach out.

NECESSARY: astray

It's true, everything is poetry. A soap dish in sudden
  larger empty space.
A little off the slant, a bit twisted and true. And hell
  yes it hurts.
The pain of. This world: Meditated and grafted.
  Kind and killing.
I suggest stronger drinks, ice and tea. How one goes
  from one to another.
To get there we need real ground, black earth. Meet at
  each accord made.
You know, when the last word's said, it'll make
  difference and negate
its not too. A beautifully vibrant setting sun. Open
  the next bottle of wine.
I would hate to see this end without dessert, so feed
  on, always
the source of. Another piece of cheese. If there were
  an easier way

I'd serve instant rice. A fable following your own
course. Say so.

Felicity in feline composure – capacious beyond the
thought.

Death only equals the doubt of give in. Fight on,
battle your charge.

VIRTUE: pray

To the lack of any god, I stop and drop to the knees of
    this.
Thought out and toughened by neglect – alone and
    creative to fill.
It can't be just. Invent courage to fool it whole. A
    generation
coming through the lack of it, we must we make us:
    A see thru
generation. Playing the jester act to court no promise.
    I
speak loud and soft whisper confusion to all ears. It's
    human,
It's eternal and void. A cross-out generation piecing
    pieces.
Break the mold broken. This is not forgive, closer to
    forgotten.
Pain feel our way in the dark and thank you for
    lighting your with me.
Oh, silly compassion silly wave of that's all and
    natural sure.

ISOLATE: hold

Sorry, seems I've lost my concentration: The real world.

Intake, fill up the tank. Armor the shield of don't. Leave -

me, alone. The next drink brings us closer, felt out the doubt.

I'll send this to you when we're read – vinyl disk the spin on.

Can you play a different speed? I meant to think but words,

words ate the way so settle for, the hope you know too kind.

Let's grave dig our future because I want not six, but four. Embedded

in the earth is our collective yes. Call, I'll write back.

Will we ever be able to sort this all out? I doubt, I trust.

Egotist rebound, ties up my thought. You were always stronger

but denied. I pass, carry clout at my side. Pause to repose.

A snap shot frozen between the ears, a yes. See ya,
   wait.
Enough of the personal, raise stakes. The world waits.
Coming to, I don't want us to go back. Solo, blank.

TORTURE: cleanse

You've racked fried my deep well slow drip world –
  put up on blocks.
A stockade of suspension, a loss of habitual ways.
  The save bounded
with the truth of, gagged with knowledge. Wisdom
  takes aim and shoots
the heart out. This blood let why. A broken arm
  resist with impossible refuse.
Some court has sentenced me to sentences, long and
  lacking. If
I could only go back to my numb days, numbing
  ways. Cross the mind out
with fuck – sleep with the soul shut, bed with the
  heart blocked. Lie
with the body and rock this stoned way home by
  doubt. Well, I we can't.
Get up – order the house. Shine that mirror.

COMPETITION: condemnation

No I swear, no it's not really in the cleavage but in the
    repeating
of some of the same words. The exact same words
    and too the splitting.
I've resigned my competency to the greater part of
    your female yes.
This rivalry in the pants is more a ravenous try to say
    than fact.
We become reactionary in division, raw upon un
    governed egg divide.
Each twin inside you, beside you. There's me and
    that's fact.
It just so happens and happens rightly so that the
    other side is waving
the same flag too. The perceived enemy talks loud
    your same words
and lovingly so. This lubricous luminary shines team
    side on.
Meet up, march out.

INDULGE: testify

Words to rhythm and the music of the beat within
   you. A light grasp.

Meaning, the beginning of hold – home the space
   between. And travel

only creates the distance, palpitations of the thought.
   Distill

the spirits here and we will cure. The art equals that
   and in us.

On two channels at least all the time: Magic
   windows.

Light up y(our) but – street pick your response,
   marshall your

resources for more than fifteen minutes, speak
   straight and say.

Lean in and stay close then pick up your scouring pad
   and clean.

We must drink in and take deep this condition, a hard
   swallow.

Apple bob the missing, elbow the rib and tap the
   inevitable.

Low hanging earrings and blue sweaters take me to
the river tonight.
Your bald spot ignites this fire. To cure to cure and
not to ask.
Why, money does your was. Your living changes the
truth on.

OBLITERATE: rhythm

Each life is heroic – other worldly ordered and so
   pain. The beat buried
deep but there. Your life a note and between scores
   the composer asks you.
Efface the daily faces., noise out both black and
   white. There are too many
to hear. Write few and listen hard, to each one. Pad
   harmony for all its worth.
You are the tonic. This key, truth.

ABSOLUTE: equals

CAOPHONY: accompaniment

You are wood block cut , core grained exposed – a
  pulp across your middle.
You lay waiting, fireplace open. The end of this and
  the thing said.
We talk of crossroads: Like silence. Tar roof heat.
It is a diversion, an excursion into the exclusion and
  rot.
I keep apolitical, hypothetical, apocalyptical,
  statemental,
resolute, evasive, mundane, scientific, clinical,
  surgical,
controversial, sure and wavering. I told you this – I
  think.
You hold up a ribboned gun, you spin my chamber,
  lick my imagery.
It can't, it must. And so. So staccato. Skip notes,
it will be O.K. This is a broad plain waiting your
  buffalo.
Familiar and foreign, forgiven and condemned –
  liberated and bound.
Your yes retrieves my make. We fish swim. We
  stroke.

FULCRUM: overboard

Failed starts of absolute envy. I Indian dance on your
   tomb, mound.
Your was includes my won't. I take air, fire, gin speak.
So she wasn't so surprised when I said I want to roll
   you up in canvas,
tie you across my tongue, roll you in wet leaves &
   honey, make
love to you on spiked wood, oil rub your head, and
   word massage your mind.
So, what's a girl to do? She said yes and surreal
   melted my poem.

We come back. Child talk green salmon days, crisp
   lettuce shorts. Bread.
Like how it's too easy to say, "I need your dough to
   rise," or "No War," "Peace."
Challenge the think said. Word fight your given.
Wrestle with your there cure.
And sure, I'll meet you half way.

Look, we all need to touch. Buy better brands. Reach across an otherwise
curious divide. Then again some of my favorite games don't have any rules. My best
friends simply exist in a nod, in a yes.

TEMPLATE: compatriot
             for the last

If I were a bit cruder, I would take notes on every inch
    of you. This read.
You reach out to several various brands of fashionable
    instruction, jean therapy.
The self hand held your own approach works best,
    when bought on time. Credit charge.
Watch out, there's a poet loose in your head. Drink a
    cigarette, smoke a line.

Sometimes what I miss is a thematic. Stay asleep, I
    need more more – cough up.
So, I wave follow, rehearse an unwritten – part words
    and part gut wrench.
Right now I want just a stroke. Inspiration or sex.
    Choose, me.
You twist inside your torn. Order hope to right care,
    feed on the fellow provider.

The difference in the method is turn. A time to call
   fish to the surface to bait

the present and cast off past. Bread the line. Soup
   for the unfed hungry.

What counts is spirit between the numbers, mass it
   up. Put on a robe and die,

your yes preaches its own demise. Thus so – raise a
   corpse then go.

This country in your woods – take axe and blaze. A
   setting son: A rising daughter.

Old men wound green with green. You take green
   too, but see green as green.

Its feminine tough. In this space of harder try, I'll see
   you. Ice pick my bye bye, freeze.

The thaw upon the you now. Pass the torch. Blaze
   on bright eye.

ABDICATE: take

You walk the boards too. Blow the match out with
  smoke, inspire this.
I miss you, you know. Wood could cut across all the
  decks, Moby wreck.
Bars do not erase the glass's hold. Take this in the
  time of. Preposition.
Act on the parts – of speech say this. This me inked
  and swollen, feather pen.
Put the word out there – single. Say, see. The feel
  between letters, right?
Phone ring the bartender's my name. Surprise of
  your dimes. Quarter this half.
If at the end of page you're still there, I do care. Sing
  your song.

ADDICTION: bliss

With you all things are possible. Possessed taken and
  sure.
I cut across the day light and write this. A thank you.
  A belief
round around the other side. Come with me past
  mythology.
Beyond the shipwrecks I stick my hand into ashes.
  Wet earth,
face fire to cool down. I want to wrap my breath
  around you.
Your love poem. A flagwave to the ahead. Branded
  and coming to.
The other half is words. Just words. Silence and full.

All equations equal
equal.
Together this
equation equals equals.
One left
out, out still.
Our us, another.
You equate
You You.

GREEN INTEGER
Pataphysics and Pedantry

Douglas Messerli, *Publisher*

Essays, Manifestos, Statements, Speeches, Maxims,
Epistles, Diaristic Notes, Narratives, Natural Histories,
Poems, Plays, Performances, Ramblings, Revelations
and all such ephemera as may appear necessary
to bring society into a slight tremolo of confusion
and fright at least.

*

Green Integer Books

1 Gertrude Stein *History, or Messages from History*
ISBN: 1-55713-354-9 $5.95
2 Robert Bresson *Notes on the Cinematographer*
ISBN: 1-55713-365-4 $8.95
3 Oscar Wilde *The Critic As Artist* ISBN: 1-55713-368-9 $9.95
4 Henri Michaux *Tent Posts* ISBN: 1-55713-328-X $10.95
5 Edgar Allan Poe *Eureka: A Prose Poem* ISBN: 1-55713-329-8 $10.95
6 Jean Renoir *An Interview* ISBN: 1-55713-330-1 $9.95
7 Marcel Cohen *Mirrors* ISBN: 1-55713-313-1 $12.95
8 Christopher Spranger *The Effort to Fall* ISBN: 1-892295-00-8 $8.95
9 Arno Schmidt *Radio Dialogs I* ISBN: 1-892295-01-6 $12.95
10 Hans Christian Andersen *Travels* ISBN: 1-55713-344-1 $12.95
11 Christopher Middleton *In the Mirror of the Eighth King*
ISBN: 1-55713-331-X $9.95